A Surprise Ending!

Children's Sermons for Lent and Easter, Cycle B

A Compilation from Children's Sermon Service Plus, a Component of SermonSuite.com

CSS Publishing Company, Inc.
Lima, Ohio

A SURPRISE ENDING!

FIRST EDITION

Library of Congress Cataloging-in-Publication Data

Title: A surprise ending! : children's sermons : for Cycle B : a compilation of "Children's Sermons" Columns from Children's Sermon Service Plus, a Component of SermonSuite.com. Description: First edition. | Lima, Ohio : CSS Publishing Company, Inc., [2020] | Summary: "A Compilation of "Children's Sermons" Columns from Children's Sermon Service Plus, a Component of SermonSuite.com"-- Provided by publisher. Identifiers: LCCN 2020049386 | ISBN 9780788030406 | ISBN 9780788030413 (ebook) Subjects: LCSH: Children's sermons. | Preaching to children. | Lenten sermons. | Eastertide--Sermons. | Common lectionary (1992). Year B.
Classification: LCC BV4315 .S87 2020 | DDC 252/.62--dc23 LC record available at https://lccn.loc.gov/2020049386

For more information about CSS Publishing Company resources, visit our website at www.csspub.com, email us at csr@csspub.com, or call (800) 241-4056.

e-book:
ISBN-13: 978-0-7880-3041-3
ISBN-10: 0-7880-3041-8

ISBN-13: 978-0-7880-3040-6
ISBN-10: 0-7880-3040-6

DIGITALLY PRINTED

Introduction

I lost count a long time ago of the number of people that have asked me what the "CSS" in CSS Publishing Company represents. The acronym has had many iterations, but essentially, CSS originally stood for Children's Sermon Service. That was our company's first product.

Our father, Wesley Runk, began writing children's sermons while still attending Hamma Divinity School at Wittenberg University in Springfield, Ohio. An entrepreneurial person by nature and with the urging of one of his parishioners, he decided to share his gift of relating the love of God among the children of his congregation with other pastors around the country.

Dad had a unique way of getting kids to respond to him. I vividly remember going up to the front of the sanctuary during worship when Dad invited all of us kids to hear a special message just for us. It was exciting to be part of this special time.

Over the years, CSS published hundreds of our father's children's sermons as a subscription and in book form. Prior to his retirement, it was determined that the mantle had to be passed down to other pastors and gifted children's writers. A long list of writers, including (but not limited to) Cynthia Cowen, Fred Steiner, Anna Shirey, Bethany Peerbolte, Arley Fadness and now John Jamison also contributed to the vast archive that now resides on SermonSuite. (I ask forgiveness of anyone whose name I've left off this list.)

Eventually, what became known as CSSPlus! was transitioned to a digital subscription service which is now a component of SermonSuite.com. The volume in your hand is a gathering of some of the best children's sermons for the Lent and Easter seasons of Cycle B. A variety of writers are represented in this collection.

My thanks go out to Rev. Bruce Batchelor-Glader for his work to compile (and edit, where needed) these offerings. We pray that these children's sermons will be a blessing to your ministry and to God's youngest and most precious gifts as they have since 1970.

In God's love and service,

David Runk, President
CSS Publishing Company, Inc.

Content

Ash Wednesday 9
Carrying God's Mark

Ash Wednesday 14
Refreshing Drink

First Sunday in Lent 16
Beloved Just As You Are

First Sunday in Lent 18
A Good Exchange (For Us)

Second Sunday in Lent 20
We Don't Have To Do This

Second Sunday in Lent 22
Faith And Grace

Third Sunday in Lent 24
God's House Is Special

Third Sunday in Lent 26
It's Smart To Love God

Fourth Sunday in Lent 28
The Little Bible

Fourth Sunday in Lent 30
Saved!

Fifth Sunday in Lent 32
A Miracle Seed

Fifth Sunday in Lent 34
Our Bridge

Liturgy of the Passion 36
A Waste Of Time?

Liturgy of the Passion 41
Name Above All Names

Maundy Thursday 43
The Last Commandment: Love One Another

Maundy Thursday 45
Remembering

Good Friday 46
Finished!

Good Friday 48
Written Down!

Resurrection of the Lord 49
A Surprise Ending

Resurrection of the Lord 53
They Saw The Resurrected Jesus

Second Sunday of Easter 55
Was It A Trick?

Second Sunday of Easter 57
God Is Light

Third Sunday of Easter 58
Dinner With God

Third Sunday of Easter 62
God's Family

Fourth Sunday of Easter 64
I Am The Good Shepherd

Fourth Sunday of Easter 66
Love By Action!

Fifth Sunday of Easter 68
Abiding in God

Fifth Sunday of Easter 71
God Is Love

Sixth Sunday of Easter 72
Jesus Chose You

Sixth Sunday of Easter 74
House Rules

Ascension of the Lord 76
Sent Out As Christ

Ascension of the Lord 80
Jesus The Head

Seventh Sunday of Easter 81
Protect Them

Seventh Sunday of Easter 83
God's Testimony

Ash Wednesday

Matthew 6:1-6, 16-21

Carrying God's Mark

Object: dark ash and oil, to mark crosses on the foreheads of the leaders (Leader 2's should be pretty light, while Leader 1's cross should be darker and more obvious).

First Thoughts: As we begin our journey into Lent, we are faced with some weighty spiritual questions. How much of our sense of faith rests on the perspective of others, and how much of it is founded on self-reflection and vulnerability to God? This is difficult for us, because we do need a spiritual community to affirm us and challenge us, and to give us a sense of our identity as Christians in the world. But when we feel our faith doesn't "count" unless it is seen by others, we run into the problems Jesus is talking about in this illustration. Are we pious in public because we want others to *think* we're holy, whether or not our private life matches up? Do we seek genuine growth and challenge from God? Is Lent just an opportunity for us to practice public humility (perhaps by declaring to anyone in earshot that we're giving up chocolate for six weeks?), or is it a chance for us to spend more time in prayer and reflection, genuinely seeking clarity and new direction from God? Reflect for a few minutes on how you will observe this Lenten season and carry that sensibility with you in your time with the children.

Props You Will Need: Dark ash and oil, to mark crosses on the foreheads of the leaders (Leader 2's should be pretty light, while Leader 1's cross should be darker and more obvious)

Teaching As A Team:

> **Leader 1:** So (name), how did you like the Ash Wednesday service tonight?
>
> **Leader 2:** It was kind of quiet and the scripture passages were a little difficult to understand, but I liked it. (really

looking at Leader 1) Hey, no fair!

Leader 1: What? What are you talking about?

Leader 2: The cross on your forehead — it's much darker than mine.

Leader 1: Does that really matter?

Leader 2: Sure it does. I mean, I went to the service just like you did. But my cross is so light people might not even see it. What's the point of having the cross if nobody can see it?

Leader 1: So you think the most important thing is to have a big black cross on your forehead so everybody can see?

Leader 2: Sure. How else will folks know that I'm ready for Lent?

Leader 1: That's a good point. But you know what? In our lesson today, Jesus says that if we're really trying to do what God wants us to do, we shouldn't make a big deal out of doing it in front of other people. Like when we pray, we shouldn't go outside and pray in a big group of people, making a show of it, because that might not be prayer at all. We might just be showing off so people think we're praying, and so they'll think we're really great.

Leader 2: You mean we're trying to impress other people instead of really talking to God?

Leader 1: Exactly. And the black cross on our foreheads isn't so other people will know we're Christians. It's to remind *us* who we are and to mark us for the Lenten journey ahead.

Leader 2: But I'm not even sure what Lent is.

Leader 1: It's the forty days before Easter. During these forty days, we're trying to walk with Christ as he walks to death on the cross and through his resurrection. It's a very special time where we look at our lives prayerfully, asking God to show us the things that aren't right in our lives, and asking God to help us make changes.

Leader 2: So even if the black cross isn't on our foreheads, it can be on our hearts?

Leader 1: That's right. In fact, that's the most important place it can be.

Teaching On Your Own: *(only a very light cross on forehead)* Hey, guys, do you see this mark on my forehead? Can you tell what it is? It's *supposed* to be a cross. I went to the Ash Wednesday service tonight, and the pastor put it on my forehead. But it's so light you can't even tell what it is. It's not fair! Some of the other people got dark crosses, ones you could really see. But not me — how will anyone know I'm a good Christian now? What do you think? Do you think having a great big black cross on my forehead is important?

That question makes me think of the lesson we have today. Jesus says that if we're really trying to do what God, wants us to do, we shouldn't make a big deal out of doing it in front of other people. Like when we pray, we shouldn't go outside and pray in a big group of people, making a show of it. That might not be prayer at all. Instead of really talking to God we might be trying to impress people about how good we are. You know what? I think that might be true of the black cross on our foreheads too. We have them not so other people will know we're good Christians, but to remind *us* who we are and to mark us for the Lenten journey ahead. Do you know what Lent is? It's the forty days before Easter. During these forty days, we're trying to walk with Christ as he walks to death on the cross and through his resurrection. It's a very special time where we look at our lives prayerfully, asking God to show us the things that aren't right in our lives, and asking God to help us make changes. So even if the black cross isn't on our foreheads, it can be on our hearts. In fact, that's the most important place it can be.

Closing Prayer: God, be with us in these forty days, as we carry your mark in our hearts and on our lives. Help us to see areas in our lives that need to be changed, and help us to bring healing and love to our families and friends. In Christ's name we pray, Amen.

Follow-Up Lesson: To reinforce this lesson at home or in a classroom setting, we're going to illustrate carrying God's mark on our hearts, through the use of paper hearts. You will either need to provide hearts or give the children a chance to cut a heart of their own out of paper. (If you want to be particularly committed to the Lenten theme, use purple paper.) Give the children a chance to think about the blessings in their lives that they're grateful for, and write a few words about these blessings on one side of a few hearts. Next, encourage the children to think of things in their lives that aren't so Christlike — things they need to change. Examples might be being grumpy in the mornings, fighting with siblings, not eating vegetables at dinner, forgetting to feed the family dog or cat, and so forth. Once they have some ideas, have them write a few words about their need for change on one side of the other hearts. Next we will mark the hearts. Provide the children with a dish of olive oil and a dish of ashes and invite them to put their finger once in the oil, then in the ash. (Make sure you have some wet wipes available for clean-up!) One by one, invite the children to make an ash cross on the back of each of their hearts. Explain to them that during Lent, these hearts will represent very special prayers of thanksgiving and of petition *(asking for help)*. The crosses on these hearts remind us of the crosses on our own hearts, which remind us that we belong to God and that God will help us. You might suggest that during the season of Lent, they can keep these hearts near their beds at night for prayer time. Or you might decide to set up a special Lenten tree for your classroom and hang the hearts there for your class reflection time in the weeks ahead. You can conclude the lesson by offering to mark the children's foreheads as well, if you would like. If you decide to mark the children's foreheads, you can say a simple prayer over each child, something like "God, be with (child's name), and give her courage and strength for him/ her journey."

Ash Wednesday

2 Corinthians 5:20b-6:10

Refreshing Drink

Object: An empty tin cup

A traveler walked across the desert and ran out of water. He got thirstier as time went on. Before long, all he could think about was getting a drink. He thought of how cool the water might be. As sweat rolled off his brow, he thought of a lovely lake and even thought he saw one straight ahead. But the lake he thought he saw was a mirage — it was a trick of the atmosphere and his eyes making him think it was a lake.

But then he saw something that was no trick. He blinked and then rubbed his eyes to make sure they were not playing a trick on him. He saw a water bucket and a tin cup, like this, just sitting there ready for him to drink. He quickly grabbed the bucket and poured the whole thing over his head. He forgot all about taking a drink. Now he had wasted all the precious water and was cooler, but still as thirsty as ever. Things did not look good for this man, because he was about to die of thirst.

I share this story with you because today is Ash Wednesday and we have an opportunity to go to God's bucket for the water of life. Today is the first day of Lent and it is a time to water our souls. Think of each week during the forty days ahead as a drink from Jesus for our souls. We don't pour it on us at once, but draw refreshment each week. It means that religion is not something we "get" at one time and then go on to other things. Instead, it means that we get a little every day. We need God's grace with each passing day, just like we need to drink water every day. We wouldn't want to waste God's grace for us.

When Paul wrote to the Corinthians he said, "We urge you not to accept the grace of God in vain." The word "vain" means empty — like the tin cup of the desert traveler.

Our prayer this Lenten season is that God would refresh our souls with the water of life — Jesus.

Dearest Lord God: Give us the water of life. Help us to accept it to refresh us. Amen.

First Sunday in Lent

Mark 1:9-15

Beloved Just As You Are

"And a voice came from heaven, 'You are my Son, the Beloved; with you I am well pleased.'" (Mark 1:11)

Good morning girls and boys,

How are you today? Good, better, or best? (Let the answer.) (Presenter chit-chats with children.)

I love to see children here at church. Of course I love to see moms and dads and others too. But your coming to worship warms my heart.

I have a couple of questions to ask you this morning.

First of all, *when* are you loved? Are you loved just as you are, or are you loved because you did a job you were asked to do? When are you loved? For example:

Do your parents say to you, "Go clean your room, and then I will love you?" (Let the answer.)

When your teachers say, "Get an A on your test, and then I will like you, even love you?"

When mom or dad says, "Go wash the dishes, and then I will love you" — is that when you are loved?

Did you know that Jesus was loved before he did anything? At about thirty years of age, Jesus began his work. At his baptism, a voice pierced the air "You are my Son the Beloved; with you I am well pleased." So before he performed a miracle, he was loved.

Before Jesus even taught the crowds he was loved.

Before Jesus healed anybody he was God's beloved.

So it is with you and me. We are loved just as we are. At your baptism into the life, death and resurrection of Jesus you are loved.

After you and I know we are loved, then we joyfully do good things for others and for God.

Next time you are asked to do something, you do it, because you know you are already loved just as you are.

Prayer: Lord Jesus, thank you for loving us just as we are. Amen.

First Sunday in Lent

1 Peter 3:18-22

A Good Exchange (For Us)

Object: Give each child a nickel or dime, with the instructions that they are to go into the congregation and exchange that coin for something else. (A variation on this is to have each child give you something for which you exchange it with something more valuable.)

Good morning! On this first Sunday in Lent, I'm going to give you something. I'm going to give you some money, and I want you to take this money and go to people in the congregation and exchange it for something else. In other words, take the nickel and ask people to give you something more valuable than a nickel. Let's see what you can get for your nickel. (Do it. You might want to prearrange this exchange with adult volunteers in the congregation who have come prepared for this exchange.)

You have just "redeemed" your money for something else. Let's see what some of you got for your nickel. (Have the children lay out their treasures. Find one item that is far more valuable than the nickel and use it for the rest of the illustration.)

You exchanged a nickel for something that is worth much more than a nickel. That is very similar to what Jesus did when he suffered and died. He gave himself to the cross so that we can have eternal life. He traded in his life and got us eternal life! Wow! That's quite a trade!

We say that Jesus "redeemed" us. By that, we mean that Jesus traded his life for ours. He laid down his life so that we can have eternal life! That is why we sometimes call Jesus "the redeemer." (You may have churches in your area named "redeemer." You can use them to illustrate the exchange Jesus made with his life.)

This time in the church year, called Lent, is a time when we look at and study why Jesus would give his life for me and for you. I wonder — why do you think he did it? (Let them answer.)

I think Jesus gave his life for us because he loves us that much!

Dearest Lord Jesus: Thank you for loving us so much that you would give your life just so we can have eternal life. Amen.

Second Sunday in Lent

Mark 8:31-38

We Don't Have To Do This

Object: Make an expression of someone who doesn't get their own way (or show a photo of someone making this expression).

Good morning, boys and girls. I'm going to make an expression on my face. (Make an expression on your face of someone who doesn't get his own way, or show a photo of someone making this expression.) Who can tell me what I'm trying to say? (Let them try to answer.) Have you ever made this expression when you wanted to do something, but someone else told you that you can't do it? You make this expression when you are not able to do what you want. Let's all try to make this expression. (Encourage the youngsters to make the expression with you.)

I want to tell you a story about a little girl who made this expression. A little girl was going to have a babysitter come to her house. When the babysitter came, the girl's parents left instructions that the girl must do some homework for a spelling test before she could have her bedtime snack.

The babysitter and the girl then began to have a good time playing with some toys. They had such a great time that they didn't realize how late it was getting. The babysitter said, "Let's stop playing and review your spelling words." The girl answered, "Oh, we're having such a good time, let's forget the spelling words. This is too much fun." The babysitter replied, "No way! We said that we'd review the spelling words. We are now going to do them. Otherwise, you will do very poorly on the test tomorrow." What expression do you think the girl made when she heard this? (Let them answer and show you the expression.)

I'm telling you this story because the same thing happened to Jesus' disciple, Peter. Jesus told his disciples that he was soon going to die. Peter stopped Jesus and said, "No, we are having too good of a time. You don't have to do this!" Jesus replied to

Peter, "Get behind me, Satan!" Jesus then told Peter that he was not thinking about the right things. Can you imagine what Peter's expression looked like? (Let them answer.)

The next time you have to do something you don't want to do, remember Jesus and Peter. Jesus came to earth for a special reason. Peter wanted Jesus to take the easy path. Jesus knew better. Jesus' answer to Peter made Peter frown.

Prayer: Jesus, you can see on our faces what we are thinking and feeling, and you love us whether we are happy or sad. Thank you for being a friend to us at all times. Amen.

Second Sunday in Lent

Romans 4:13-25

Faith And Grace

Good morning! Today we hear about two words that are popular in church. They are words we use all the time, but we may not know the meaning of them. The two words I'm speaking of are GRACE and FAITH. How many of you have heard those words in church before? (Let them answer.) How many heard the word "grace" already this morning? (Let them answer.) How about the word "faith"? (Let them answer.)

To show you what they mean, I need a volunteer. Would someone be willing to be the person with FAITH? (Have one of the children volunteer.) What I want you to do is stand in front of me, facing away from me. Now, I want you to have FAITH. I want you to fall straight backward. Don't try to catch yourself. Let yourself fall. Are you willing to do that? (Let the child answer.) Okay — let's do it. (Do it.)

It took faith on your part to fall straight backward. You would have hurt yourself if I hadn't caught you. When you trust someone so much that you know they won't let you get hurt, that's called "faith," and you just showed us all what faith is.

Now, your faith was in a person. Your faith was in me. I also had to do my part to keep you from getting hurt. I could have been really mean and let you fall and hurt yourself, and then maybe even laugh at you. But I didn't do that. I showed that I was FAITH-worthy. I showed that I had GRACE. I caught you!

That second word, GRACE, means to have a loving attitude toward another person. It means to love another unconditionally. In a sense, I showed GRACE this morning by lovingly catching you when you fell.

God is full of GRACE. God loves us all. God loves us, no matter what! God is trustworthy — FAITH-worthy. We know we can trust God; we can have FAITH in God because of God's GRACE.

When we use these words, faith and grace, perhaps you will know more about what they mean. Who knows the story about Abraham and Sarah? (Let them answer.) In this lesson we have today, the apostle Paul tells about how Abraham and Sarah had faith in God's grace. Even though Abraham and Sarah were very old, God had promised them a son, and God showed God's grace by giving them a son. They had faith in trusting God.

Dearest God: Give us more faith in your grace. Amen.

Third Sunday in Lent

John 2:13-22

God's House Is Special

Good morning, boys and girls. It seems like a special day to me today. Does it seem special to you? (let them answer) I guess every time I come to church, the day seems special. I really look forward to seeing you every Sunday, you make it special for me.

I wonder if any of you brought with you today the things I brought with me. (Open your bag and take out the items one by one.) Did anyone here bring their soap, washcloth, and towel? (Let them answer.) You didn't? Is that why I can't find the water that I need? Isn't this the place where you wash your face and hands? (Let them answer.) This isn't the place? Maybe I could brush my teeth here! I have my toothbrush and toothpaste. Would this be a good place? (Let them answer.) This isn't a good place for brushing your teeth? Has anyone seen a mirror? (Let them answer.) I have my comb, and I thought I would make sure that my hair was combed correctly. I suppose this isn't the place to comb my hair. Where do you comb your hair, brush your teeth, and wash your face and hands? (Let them answer.) The bathroom! That's the place you do these things. So you never come to church to brush your teeth, comb your hair, or wash your face and hands? (Let them answer.) Now, I understand.

The reason that I did this was to get you ready to hear a story about Jesus. Jesus went to church one day and he saw something that really upset him. He came to church so that he could pray and read from the scriptures. But instead, there were a lot of people doing other things. They were selling animals like doves, sheep, and cattle. There was a lot of money being used and making noise. Do you think it would be pretty noisy in here if there were sheep, cows, donkeys, and birds and everyone yelling at the top of their voices, "Two doves for the price of one?" Or maybe someone would say, "Buy your sheep here, fine wool, healthy, no defects or blemishes." Would you like to try to pray and sing hymns with someone yelling, "Special sale on all cows with black eyes and floppy ears"? (Let them answer.) I don't think so. And neither did Jesus. He told the people that God's house was a place for worship, and not a place to sell animals or anything else.

This isn't a place to wash your face and hands, brush your teeth, comb your hair, or sell doves, sheep, and cattle. Jesus said anyone wanting to do these things should find another place. He told them this was God's house.

So the next time you take out your toothbrush, remember where you should brush your teeth and at the same time remember why you come to church. God's church is a place of prayer, singing hymns, and reading the scriptures.

Prayer: Thank you, God, for this church, this special place where we can sing, pray, and love you and each other. Thank you for your house. Amen.

Third Sunday in Lent

1 Corinthians 1:18-25

It's Smart To Love God

Good morning, boys and girls. I want to ask you a question. Is there anyone here who thinks that he/she is as smart as God? (Let them answer.) No one here thinks they are as intelligent as God. Kind of disappointing, isn't it? How many of you think your mom or dad is as smart as God? (Let them answer.) You don't think your mom or dad is as smart as God either? Do you suppose if we added up everything that everyone who is attending church today knows and put it all together, that we would be as smart as God? (Let them answer.) You don't think all of us together are as smart as God? Let's ask one more question. What if we took all of the teachers and professors in the whole world and put them together in the same building. Would they be as smart as God? (Let them answer.) You don't think so?

I think we'd better get busy, don't you? I brought along some books that I would like to have you read this week. I need some volunteers. I have a book on medicine. Who would like to read it? (See if anyone volunteers.) Then I have this big one that lawyers read, and I also have one that our banker keeps on his bookshelf. Has anyone ever read the dictionary? Would someone like to read this one, while someone else reads my encyclopedia? Now if we read all of these books this week, we should be as smart as God is, don't you think? (Let them answer.) You don't think so.

Guess what? You are right. But you know God isn't really worried about how smart you are. God isn't giving tests. He doesn't ask us to know everything about medicine, law, banking, or anything. What God really wants us to do is believe that Jesus died for our sins so that we can join God in living a good life.

It is good to learn and to learn as many things as we can. God has given us a brain and a curiosity so that we want to know more about the world in which we live. But God also gave us a spirit so that we could be like him. The problem is that some people believe that being real smart will fix everything. But there is something called sin, that gets in the way and keeps us from really knowing God.

The secret to a good life is this: Believe that Jesus came and died for our sins. When we believe that Jesus is our Savior, then our sin goes away and we live a good life with God. It is easy, so simple that sometimes we try to make it more difficult.

So the Bible teaches us that it is not how much we know, but how much we love Jesus and believe in him that makes the difference. The next time you see a big book, you can remember that God isn't giving tests on how much we know, but instead that he shared his love with us in Jesus.

Prayer: It is good to be smart, but it is even better to be loved. Thank you, God, for showing us your love through Jesus. Help us to love one another. Amen.

Fourth Sunday in Lent

John 3:14-21

The Little Bible

Object: Paper heart inscribed with John 3:16 and inserted in center of a Bible

> *"For God so loved the world He gave his only Son, so that everyone who believes in him may not perish but may have eternal life."*
> (John 3: 16)

Good morning girls and boys,

Thanks for joining me this morning. I have something to show you, and something to tell you.

I have here a book, in fact it's the best book in the entire world. What is it? (Children respond.)

Yep, it's the Holy Bible. I'll bet you have one of these in your home. (Children respond.)

Now when I open this Bible, there is something inside it. Know what it is? (Children guess.) (Presenter opens the Bible.) Look what I found. I found a heart. And written on the heart are these words: "For God so loved the world he gave his only Son, so that everyone who believes in him may not perish but may have eternal life." That's John 3:16.

Martin Luther called John 3:16 the heart of the Bible. John 3:16 is the Bible in miniature, the Bible made tiny. In other words, everything that is most important in the Bible is found in John 3:16. Isn't that amazing? A tiny Bible in the big Bible.

And so, beloved children, will you repeat after me:

For God (Children repeat.) The Bible is all about God.

So loved (Children repeat.) The Bible tells us God loves the world — everybody and everything.

God gave God's only Son (Children repeat.) God gave Jesus to die for us.

So we may have eternal life (Children repeat.) We get a new life now and forever as believers in Jesus.

A song we sing about this is "Jesus loves me this I know for the Bible tells me so."

Let's sing this song. (Presenter leads children in singing.)

Prayer: Dear Lord in heaven, thank you for John 3:16. Thank you for this tiny Bible. In just a few words, it shows us of your divine love and grace in Jesus. Thank you. Amen.

Fourth Sunday in Lent

Ephesians 2:1-10

Saved!

Object: A rope

I brought some rope with me this morning to help me tell a story. The story is about a boy about your age whose name was Robert. Robert went with some friends to a place his mother had told him not to go near — the river. It was usually a calm river — but deep. This day, however, was different. The water was high and flowing swiftly because of the melting snow upstream. Robert and his friends loved putting floating things in the river to see how fast the water would take them away. Robert found a large log but he struggled to get it to the river and put it in. Then it happened. He slipped and fell right into the rushing waters. How do you think Robert felt? (Let them answer.)

Robert was scared. He was also very cold because the waters were so cold from the melting snows. But Robert was so scared he scarcely noticed how cold the waer was as the rushing river took him off, just like the log Robert had tried so hard to put in the river.

Luck would have it that a man was watching the river downstream and saw what happened. He heard the shouts of the boys and heard Robert's calls for help. The man ran to a docked boat and pulled a rope like this from it. As the river swept Robert by him, he got Robert's attention and threw the rope to him. The rope landed just within reach and Robert grabbed it, and the man pulled him to safety. Robert's life was spared by the man and his rope.

The next day at school, Robert told his classmates about his adventure in the river. He told about how he had accidentally fallen in and the swift river carried him away. But then Robert bragged about how he calmly swam to shore (even though Robert didn't know how to swim) and saved himself.

This story is a lot like how God saves us. We are carried away by sin and death and then God throws us a rope that saves us. We call that rope "grace" and that is what makes us safe. We, like Robert, do not save ourselves. We are saved by God who loves us and does what he must to save us.

Dear God: Thank you for saving us by grace. Amen.

Fifth Sunday in Lent

John 12:20-33

A Miracle Seed

Object: Scruffy container filled with soil and a flower seed

> *"Very truly I tell you, unless a grain of wheat falls into the earth and dies, it remains just a single fruit; but if it dies, it bears much fruit."* (John 12:24)

Good morning boys and girls,

I have a question. Does anybody know what month we are in, and what day it is today?

(Children answer — March and the date.)

You're right, and do you know what happened yesterday?

(Children may have no clue.) Yesterday was the first day of spring! And spring means planting.

Planting gardens, fields, and flowers. Oh, what fun. I hope you get to plant something sometime this spring.

I have here a container and a seed, and I'm going to throw away this seed by burying it in this dirty old dirt. (Throws plant seed carelessly.) But children you know what's going to happen? This seed that I'm trying to get rid of — with some water and tender love, will pop up out of the dirt into a beautiful flower.

Jesus told his followers after they arrived in Jerusalem, he would be like that. When a seed is buried and dies it will grow and pop up into many beautiful seeds. Jesus meant that *he* would die and be buried but be raised up from the dead. And then he and his believers would be many.

So the next time you get to plant something, think about Jesus. After a period of time, you will have a wonderful vegetable or flower, grass, or even a grain.

What would you like to plant this spring? (Children answer.)

(Option: Here are packets of seeds for each of you to plant) Have fun and remember a seed is like Jesus — buried, but rose from the dead.

Prayer: Dear Jesus, though your disciples did not understand what was going to happen to you in Jerusalem, we get it. We know what happened and today thank you for saving us from sin and the devil. Amen.

Fifth Sunday in Lent

Hebrews 5:5-10

Our Bridge

Object: Popsicle sticks (or other small, straight object to represent a bridge).

Good morning! Today, we read that Jesus is a "priest forever." What is a priest? (Let them answer.) Perhaps the best way to describe a priest is to say that a priest stands between us and God. There is an old Latin word for priest that is the same word as "bridge." A priest is like a bridge between us and God. Let's pretend this popsicle stick is a bridge. God is here, and we are here. Jesus comes between us and God.

How is Jesus a priest? (Let them answer.) Jesus formed a bridge between us and God when he died on the cross and rose from the grave. Before Jesus did that, there was a big gap between us and God. God seemed so far away. But Jesus brought God closer to us and us closer to God.

So Jesus is our priest because Jesus makes it possible for us to get to God and for God to reach us. There is something else Jesus does. Not only does Jesus become like a bridge between us and God, but Jesus is also like a bridge from us to other people. (At this, lay the other popsicle stick over the other, forming a cross.)

I guess you could say that the cross reminds us that Jesus is a bridge from us to God and from God to us, as well as a bridge from ourselves to others and from others to ourselves. That's a neat way of thinking about the cross, isn't it? Let's glue these two sticks together here this morning to remind us of our priest — our bridge — Jesus. Next Sunday, I will wear this cross around my neck, to help us all remember that Jesus is our priest — forever. (If you say this, you must do it. Let the glue dry and then fix the cross so that you can wear it next Sunday.)

Dearest God: Thank you for sending Jesus as our bridge — our priest. Amen.

Mark 14:1-15:47

A Waste Of Time?

First Thoughts: The assigned lectionary reading for Passion Sunday is very long and full of powerful lessons for Easter. We're going to focus on this first story in the passage (Mark 14:1-9), about the woman who anoints Jesus with the expensive ointment. Have you ever found yourself the recipient of a truly lavish gift — one that not only cost the giver (in time, energy, money) but one that truly responded to your needs? How did it feel to receive that gift? On the other hand, have you ever felt motivated to give another person a lavish gift? How did you feel about offering such a gift? Excited, hesitant, confident, insecure? It's not uncommon for some people to hold off in the offering of lavish gifts, since doing so makes us vulnerable. What if our gift isn't appreciated or even rejected? When we offer someone a gift from the heart, we're really offering the heart itself. And when we do that, we have the same Spirit that motivated Jesus in his life — a love that risks everything and trusts in its own power to persevere. Spend a few moments reflecting on your own willingness to live in this love and carry your prayerful attention to your time with the children.

Props You Will Need: none

Teaching As A Team:

(Leader 2 comes in looking tired.)

> **Leader 1:** Hey, (name). You look kind of tired. Been busy lately?
>
> **Leader 2:** Yes. Yesterday was my mom's birthday and I spent *all day* getting ready.
>
> **Leader 1:** Wow! What did you do?

Leader 2: I know my mom loves carrot cake, so I decided to make one from scratch. I grated all the carrots and chopped up all the nuts, I even made the frosting myself.

Leader 1: That's a lot of work but that probably shouldn't have taken all day.

Leader 2: No, but then I remembered that she really likes fresh flowers. So I went across town to my aunt's garden and picked her a nice bouquet of flowers. That took a couple of hours. And then I needed a gift.

Leader 1: What did you come up with?

Leader 2: I made her a scrapbook with all of my baby pictures. That took a long time — finding the pictures, putting them in the book, and making it look nice.

Leader 1: So you really did take all day, didn't you?

Leader 2: Yeah (looks thoughtful for a moment), do you think I spent *too much* time on it?

Leader 1: Why do you ask?

Leader 2: Well, my friends called in the morning to ask me to play soccer, and then in the afternoon to invite me to go for ice cream. I told them I was busy working on my mom's birthday, and they told me I had wasted my whole day.

Leader 1: I don't agree with your friends. You spent your day making gifts of love and that's never a waste of time. Our story today tells us about a woman who gave a gift of love to Jesus. Jesus was eating dinner at a friend's house, and the woman came in with a very expensive bottle of perfume. She broke it open and poured it on Jesus' feet. She gave the very best thing she had to show Jesus how much she loved him. But not everyone thought it was a good thing.

Leader 2: Why not?

Leader 1: Because some of them had the same idea as your friends: they thought she had wasted that perfume. She could have used it for something else or even sold it to raise money to help feed poor people. But Jesus told them that she had done the right thing. You don't have to "save" your love or keep it for a rainy day. Love is amazing because the more you give it, the more you have. And Jesus really needed that love too, since in just a few days he was going to die on the cross.

Leader 2: But I don't understand. What good did her love do, if he ended up dying anyway?

Leader 1: I'm sure it encouraged him to be faithful when he was scared, and it helped him to offer love even to the people who were hurting him. Love is a pretty powerful thing. Giving and receiving love makes us stronger.

Leader 2: (flexing muscles) You know what? I do feel kinda pumped up today.

Leader 1: (feeling muscles) Yeah and I bet your mom does too!

On Your Own: Hey, guys! Boy, am I tired today. Yesterday was my mom's birthday, and I spent all day getting ready. First I made her favorite carrot cake from scratch! Then I went across town to my aunt's house and picked her a bouquet of flowers. Then I decided that, for a gift, I would put together a scrapbook of all my baby pictures. I started in the morning and didn't get done until late afternoon. That's a long time, huh? Do you think it was *too* long? My friends do. They called me in the morning to see if I could play soccer, then again in the afternoon to see if I wanted to go out for ice cream. I told them I was busy, and they said I had wasted my whole day on something that wasn't really important. What do you think? Do you think I wasted my day? I don't think so. You know why? Because I was giving my mom gifts of love, and I don't think love is ever a waste of time. Our story today tells us about a woman who gave a gift of love to Jesus. Jesus was eating dinner at a friend's house, and the woman came in with a very expensive bottle of perfume. She broke it open and poured it on Jesus' feet. She gave the very best thing she had, to show Jesus how much she loved him. But not everyone thought it was a good thing. Some of them thought she was wasting the perfume. They said she could have used it for something else or even sold it to raise money to help feed poor people. But Jesus told them that she had done the right thing. You don't have to "save" your love or keep it for a rainy day. Love is amazing because the more you give it, the more you have. And Jesus really needed that love too, since in just a few days he was going to die on the cross. I'm sure it encouraged him to be faithful when he was scared, and it helped him to offer love even to the people who were hurting him. Love is a pretty powerful thing. Giving and receiving love makes us stronger. (flexing muscles) And you know what? I do feel kinda pumped up today, and I bet my mom does too!

Closing Prayer: Creator God, you who created love and grows love in us, help us to be courageous and faithful in sharing our love with others. Help us to always know that love is never a waste of time, love believes all things, hopes all things, and endures all things. When we live in love, we live in you. In Christ's name we pray, Amen.

Follow-Up Lesson: A good way to follow up this lesson in a home or classroom setting is to spend more time talking about the lasting power of love. To do this lesson, you will need palm branches and heart ornaments (porcelain, metal, or some other hard material). Start with reviewing the Palm Sunday liturgy (Mark 11:1-11), since many churches include the palm processional as part of this Sunday's worship. Talk about how the crowd gathered around, shouting "Hosanna!" and waving palms. Then ask the question: They were praising Jesus, but did they offer love? Why or why not? Now revisit the story of the woman with the perfume. How is what she offered different than the crowd? What they offered was cheap and inconsistent. It didn't cost them much, and that same crowd was gone when Jesus was arrested. What the woman offered came from her heart, and her gift of love went with Jesus and gave him strength through his trial and death.

Give each child a palm branch and a heart ornament. What is the difference between the two? The palm branch will soon wilt and fall to pieces, but the ornament will last. Help the children think of the difference between "palm branch" love and "heart" love. (Examples: fair-weather friends versus forever friends, giving food to the food bank you don't like versus giving up your favorite cereal.) As a part of the lesson, invite the children to write on their hearts a paraphrase from 1 Corinthians 13:8a; "Love never ends." If you have a Lent tree, invite each child to write their name on the ornaments and hang them on the tree. Otherwise, send the hearts home with them.

Philippians 2:5-11

Name Above All Names

Good morning, boys and girls. Do any of you have stuffed animals or dolls that you have named? (Let them answer.) This morning I brought (give the name and explain what the toy is). It's fun to name toys.

I want to tell you about a girl your age, who had some stuffed animals and some dolls. She also had a cat. It was very important to this girl that all of these toys and her cat had names. Names tell us so much about something. She took her time, and thought and thought about good names for everything. Finally, she named her cat Midnight. What color do you suppose her cat was? (Let them answer.) She named one of her stuffed animals Teddy. What kind of a stuffed animal do you think Teddy was? (Let them answer.) She had another stuffed animal that was green. She named it Kermit. What kind of stuffed animal do you think Kermit was? (Let them answer.) You are all very good at this! She had another important toy, which had long hair and wore a dress, which she named Sarah. What kind of toy do you think Sarah was? (Let them answer.) There were many other toys and dolls that she named. After she named them all, she felt very good.

Just as the little girl named her toys and dolls, our parents gave us important names. There is one other person who has an important name that I want to tell you about. That person is Jesus. Our lesson this morning tells us that God gave Jesus the name that is above every name. God gave Jesus such an important name that everyone in heaven and on earth should bow before him and should say that Jesus Christ is Lord.

The next time you have a new pet, or doll or stuffed animal, I know that you will give it a name. When you name it, remember that God gave Jesus the name that is above all names. Jesus is Lord.

Prayer: Thank you, God, for knowing each one of our names and for giving your love the name of Jesus, in whose name we pray. Amen.

Maundy Thursday

John 13:1-17, 31b-35

The Last Commandment: Love One Another

"I give you a new commandment, that you love one another. Just as I have loved you, you also should love one another" (John 13: 34).

Object: Baptismal font/bowl of water.

Good morning boys and girls,

I have a quiz for you this morning (this evening). Are you ready for a fun quiz?

When I say "I love you", what makes you believe that I really do love you?

When I give a speech about love to you?

When I define love from the dictionary?

When I tell a story about love?

When I reach over and hug you?

Yes, when I reach over and hug you, that proves that I love you.

Actions are better than just words.

So it is the night of Jesus' betrayal. Jesus and his twelve disciples are having their last supper together.

Normally servants serve and wash the feet of the guests. Because feet are dusty and sweaty in that culture, it feels wonderful to have one's feet washed and refreshed.

But no one washes the disciple's feet. No servants. Not Peter. Nor John. Not any of the disciples. Surely not Judas Iscariot, who would betray Jesus later.

So Jesus got up and took the bowl, like this one, and washed the disciples' feet. And then Jesus said, "I give you a new commandment, that you love one another, just as I have loved you."

Actions are more powerful than words aren't they? Now, who will volunteer to have their feet washed tonight? Be brave. When I wash your feet, my washing says I really do love you. Deep and true love is not only saying "I love you", but by doing wonderful loving things for you. And then you and I should love others.

Prayer: Dear loving Jesus, you showed the disciples and us how to love. Give us not only words about love, but gives us directions for how to love others. Amen.

Maundy Thursday

1 Corinthians 11:23-26

Remembering

Object: Small piece of string.

Today, I brought a piece of string. Why would I bring a piece of string to this worship service? Does anybody have any ideas? (Let them answer.) Sometimes people use a piece of string tied around their fingers to help them remember something. Tonight, I want to remember something very, very important. I want to remember Jesus and what he did on this night a long time ago. Do you think a piece of string is a good way to remember what happened on Holy Thursday? (Let them answer.)

Maybe I don't need a piece of string to remember! After all, I have the bread and the wine of the Lord's Supper to remind me. He took the bread and prayed a prayer of thanks. Then he broke it and said to the disciples, "This is my body, which is for you." He said to do this to remember him.

Then he took the cup and said, "This cup is the new covenant in my blood. Do this, as often as you drink it, in remembrance of me." The cup of wine would also remind Jesus' followers what it was all about. I'm a follower of Jesus and this same cup and loaf of bread remind me also that Jesus suffered and died for me. How could I ever forget Jesus and all that Jesus did — *for me!*

Jesus died for you as well. We have the bread and wine of the Lord's supper to remind us that Jesus loved us so much that he went to the cross for us. He must have really loved us!

Dearest Lord: Thank you for loving us so much and giving us something to remember you by. Amen.

Good Friday

John 18:1-19:42

Finished!

"When Jesus had received the wine, he said, 'It is finished.' Then he bowed his head and gave up his spirit."

Good morning boys and girls,

Who of you likes to color? What is your favorite color? (Children respond.)

My favorite color is ________ and here's the reason why__________________.

I have here a coloring book/picture, but it's not finished. *(show picture)* See, there is just one little item to color in. Let's finish it. What color shall we use? (Children respond.)

(Presenter or selected child finishes the picture.) Now, that looks wonderful. Let's all celebrate and say together, it is finished! ***It is finished.*** (Show the congregation, invite applause.)

One of the last things Jesus said on the cross just before he died was, "It is finished."

What did Jesus mean when he said 'it is finished?"

Was Jesus' suffering finished? Did Jesus finish keeping God's holy law?

Did Jesus finish fulfilling the prophecies? Did Jesus finish the work of salvation?

Whatever Jesus meant, he did the most wonderful thing – he finished saving us from our sins. He finished offering himself so we may be given eternal life. His purpose was all done, complete. That's why this cross is so precious to us. (Show a cross.)

Are there things in your life that need to be finished? Like finishing a school assignment? Finish reading a book? Finish a chore? Finish showing love to a bullied friend?

When you and I finish something, we remember the greatest task in the world was finished by Jesus on that first Good Friday.

So today on this Good Friday, we are sad — but we are glad. It's finished! Saved from our sins — this is Good News!! Let's tell our friends and everybody.

Prayer: Jesus you did it all. You saved us. You finished the work. Thank you. Amen.

Good Friday

Hebrews 10:16-25

Written Down!

Object: paper and pencil/pen

God says that a day is coming when he will put his laws in people's hearts, and will write them in people's minds. How do you suppose God will do this? Will God take a piece of paper, like this, and a pencil and then write down the laws God makes up and then stuff them inside people's heads? (Let them answer.)

If God doesn't do that, how does God get the message across? How does God speak to us so that we can know what God wants? How can we hear what God wants to tell us, and make what we hear a part of who we are? Those were the kinds of questions God had about us. God answered those questions in a very ingenious way. God himself became God's own word. God became a person. The person God became, we call... (Let them answer.) We call Jesus God's word made flesh.

When Jesus did something on this day long ago, it helped us remember God's word, God's message to us. What did Jesus do on this day? (Let them answer.) Jesus died on the cross. By doing that, God's word became a part of us. God was able to write his word in our hearts and minds.

And what is God's word to us? (Let them answer.) It is the word of love. God loves us. We know that, because Jesus went all the way to the cross to tell us that word. That word of God's love for each of us is now in our hearts (make a motion around the heart) and our minds (use hand motions here, too).

So Jesus is part of us, because God's word fills us. What Jesus did on the cross speaks to us better than any word spoken with the mouth could speak.

Dearest Lord Jesus: Thank you for dying on the cross for us. You tell us of God's love and we thank you for that love. Amen.

Resurrection of the Lord

John 20:1-18

A Surprise Ending

Object: None

First Thoughts: This story is so familiar to us we might not recognize the resurrection as a surprise ending. In fact, we'd be surprised if the story didn't end this way. But we need to be aware of the revolutionary message of hope the resurrection illumines for us. We can't reduce it to a theological formula, although theologians have tried for centuries. No, this is an encounter with mystery, the same mystery that interacts with us today, which turns over our expectations and delivers to us something we never could have foreseen. Think of a time in your life when everything seemed to flip over. Your plans were unhinged, a relationship fell apart, a beloved died. Looking back on that time, can you identify a divine reversal? A moment where God asserted his love and resurrected your old life to bring you something new? This is the real power and lesson of resurrection, because God has the power to see beyond our losses, to envision for us a future when we can't even see beyond our feet. God is always doing the new thing in our lives and in the world. So rejoice and welcome the surprise!

Props You Will Need: None

Teaching As A Team:

> **Leader 1:** I'm going to tell you a little story this morning.
>
> **Leader 2:** Oh, great. I love stories.
>
> **Leader 1:** This is the story of three little pigs. They each went out in the world to seek their fortunes, and each one built a house. Once the houses were done, in came the Big Wolf, and he knocked on the first pig's door and said,

Leader 2: "Little pig, little pig, let me come in!"

Leader 1: But the pig said,

Leader 2: "Not by the hair on my chinny chinny chin."

Leader 1: So the wolf said,

Leader 2: "Then I'll huff and I'll puff and I'll blow your house in."

Leader 1: Wrong. The wolf said, "Oh, please let me come in. It's cold outside and I'm getting hungry." So the little pig brought him in to sit at the fire and made him some oatmeal. The end.

Leader 2: That's not how the story goes.

Leader 1: That's how *this* story goes. See, it has a surprise ending. You thought something else was going to happen and you almost missed the story. That's the same thing that happened to Jesus' friends.

Leader 2: What do you mean?

Leader 1: Remember, Jesus' friends saw that Jesus was arrested and killed on the cross and then they saw Jesus buried in the tomb. What do you think they thought after seeing all that?

Leader 2: Sad, because Jesus was gone.

Leader 1: That's right. They thought this was the end of the story. The women even came to the tomb to take care of his body, still crying as they walked. But when they got to the tomb...

Leader 2: A surprise ending!

Leader 1: That's right. The tomb was open and Jesus' body wasn't there. Jesus' friend Mary was confused but she was determined to figure out what was going on. She looked into the tomb and saw two angels, all in white. Then she turned around and saw another man...

Leader 2: Jesus!

Leader 1: That's right, but she still didn't recognize him. She was still stuck in that first ending. But when he said her name, that's when she knew Jesus was alive.

Leader 2: She must have been so excited!

Leader 1: I'm sure she was. Easter is a good reminder to us that, just when we think we've figured everything out, God can surprise us!

Leader 2: I guess when things seem really scary and dark, the best thing we can do is just be patient and let God write our stories.

Leader 1: Yep, let God surprise us.

Teaching On Your Own: I'm going to tell you guys a little story this morning. Once upon a time, there were three little pigs that set out to make their fortunes in the world. Each pig built himself a house and once the houses were done, in came the Big Wolf. He knocked on the first pig's door and said (Encourage the kids to say it with you), "Little pig, little pig, let me come in!" But the little pig said (Again encouraging kids to say it together), "Not by the hair on my chinny chinny chin." So the wolf said (see if some kids will spontaneously fill in the blanks without you — if not, ask them "What do you think he said?" Kids' line: "Then I'll huff and I'll puff and I'll blow your house in.") Wrong! The wolf said, "Oh, please let me come in. It's cold outside and I'm getting hungry." So the little pig brought him in to sit at the fire and made him some oatmeal. The end. Is this a different story than what you expected? It has a surprise ending, doesn't it? You thought you knew what the ending was, so you almost didn't hear the new ending. That's the same thing that happened to Jesus' friends in our lesson today. What had happened to Jesus? Jesus was arrested and killed on the cross and then buried in the tomb. His friends saw that. What do you imagine they were thinking? They thought this was the end of the story. The women even came to the tomb to take care of his body, still crying as they walked. But when they got to the tomb, they found a surprise ending. The tomb was open and Jesus' body wasn't there. Jesus' friend Mary was confused but she was determined to figure out what was going on. She looked into the tomb and saw two angels all in white. Then she turned around and saw another man. Who do you think the man was? Jesus! But she still didn't recognize him. She was still stuck in that first ending. But when he said her name, that's when she knew Jesus was alive. Easter is a good reminder to us that, just when we think we've figured everything out, God can surprise us! The lesson of Easter is that sometimes, when things seem the darkest, all we can do is be patient and let God write our stories. Let God surprise us.

Closing Prayer: Loving God, thank you for your surprise endings. Give us hearts that are ready and waiting for your surprises and help us share your surprises with the world. Help us to live the lesson of Easter each day. Help us to realize that you are doing a new thing, if we only have eyes and ears to perceive it. In Christ's name we pray, Amen.

1 Corinthians 15:1-11

They Saw The Resurrected Jesus

Object: A box with a picture of some well-known member of your congregation in it and the number 525 written in large numbers on a large piece of paper

Alternative: Place an easily identifiable picture of Jesus in the box instead of the church member

Good morning, boys and girls. Today I have something very special in a box. (Select a volunteer.) Do you promise not to say anything until I say it is all right? (Let them answer.) Good. (open the box just wide enough for the volunteer to see the picture.) Did you see it? (Let them answer.) *You won't tell anyone, will you?* (Let them answer.)

Would anyone else like to take a look and promise not to tell? (Take each child, one at a time and after each one looks in the box, make them promise not to tell what they saw.) Very good! Well, everyone has looked and no one has told anyone what they saw, is that right? (Let them answer.) That's great!

Is it possible that we really all saw the same thing? (begin with the first one again and ask the person to say out loud what he/she really saw). Everyone saw a picture. *Does anyone know the person in the picture?* (Let them answer.) *Could it have been anyone else?* (Let them answer.) *You are positive that the person in the picture was ________________. If just one of you said it was ______________, there might be a question of who it really was. If only two of you looked in the box and said that it was the picture of ______________, I might think that both of you were wrong, but when everyone says the picture is of _________________, then I have to believe that you are all good witnesses.*

(take out the big number 525) *Can anyone here tell me what this number is?* (Let them answer.) Do you know what that number means? (Let them answer.) It means that about 525 people saw Jesus after he died, was buried and rose again from the tomb. The apostle Paul says that it could have been more, but he knows that Cephas (*we call him Peter*) saw Jesus, and then the twelve disciples saw Jesus, and then at least 500 people saw Jesus, then James and then the disciples again, and finally Paul saw him also. Add it up and it comes to 525 or more people who saw Jesus after he died and rose again from the dead. We believe [number of children who looked in the box] people who said they saw __________ in a picture. If we believed them, should we believe 525 or more? I think so, and so does most of the world. We are so glad Jesus came back from the dead so that all of us can believe.

Prayer: Jesus, thank you for coming back to life on Easter and for taking the time to visit so many of your friends. Help us to see you in every person that we meet. Help us to share your love with the world. Amen.

Second Sunday of Easter

John 20:19-31

Was It A Trick?

Object: a deck of cards for a card trick

Good morning! After Jesus was raised from the dead, he appeared to his disciples. One of the disciples named Thomas, was not there when Jesus came and he didn't believe that Jesus had really shown himself to them. Later, Jesus came back and appeared again, and Thomas was there. When he saw Jesus, he believed, but Jesus said to him, "Blessed are those who have not seen and yet have come to believe."

If you have faith, you believe without having to see. Let me show you what I mean by that. Here is a deck of cards. I can have you pick out a card from this deck, keep me from seeing it, and put it back in the deck. Then, even after I shuffle the cards, I can tell you which card you picked. How many of you believe that I can do that? (Let them answer.) Okay, those who think I can do it, have faith. The rest of you have to see me do it before you will believe. You're just like Thomas, who wouldn't believe until he saw with his own eyes.

Okay, Let's do it. (*Do the trick as it is explained below.)

Now, you all believe I can do it because you saw it done. Jesus says that God blesses those who believe without seeing. Do you all believe in Jesus as your Lord and Savior? (Let them answer.) That's good! You are blessed then, because you believe in him even though you have not seen him. Let's thank God for giving us faith so that we can believe.

Dear God: We thank you for giving us faith so that we can believe in Jesus even though we have not seen him. Amen.

***Card Trick Explanation:** use a deck with pictures and arrange them in advance so they all face the same way. When they draw a card and look at it, make sure they put it back the opposite way, so that when you go through the deck, you will immediately spot that particular card. Shuffling will not change this as long as you shuffle with each part of the deck facing the same way.

Second Sunday of Easter

1 John 1:1-2:2

God Is Light

Object: nightlight" at the beginning of this sermon

Good morning, boys and girls. Are any of you afraid of the dark? (Let them answer.) I think just about everyone in this church was afraid of the dark at one time. How many of you have a night light to help you sleep at night? (Let them answer and show the night light.)

I want to tell you about a little girl, about your age who was afraid of the dark. When she went to bed at night she would cry, "Please turn on the light, I'm afraid." Then someone would come to her room and turn on a lamp, or her closet light or the hall light. Has that ever happened to any of you? (Let them answer.)

Her parents wanted to help her get to sleep. So, they bought a night light, like this one. They put it in her room. She was able to turn it on herself at night. Her night light had a warm glow to it that really made her feel safe. Whenever she went to bed from then on, she had no problem getting to sleep because she felt safe with her night light.

This night light makes me think of God. In this morning's lesson, the Bible says that God is light and in him there is no darkness at all. The Bible says that when we walk in the light, we are walking like other Christians. When I think of God being like this night light, I think of God spreading a light over a world of darkness. So, tonight when you go to bed, remember to turn on your night light. If you don't have one, someone probably turns on a lamp or a hall light for you. Remember that God is like a night light. In God, there is no darkness at all.

Prayer: God, shine your light into our lives so that we can always feel safe in its glowing. Help us to be your light for the world. Amen.

Third Sunday of Easter

Luke 24:36b-48

Dinner With God

First Thoughts: Here we have another one of these miraculous revelation stories, where Jesus appears to his friends post-resurrection and they respond with fear and wonder. When we think about it, though, aren't our lives full of God's revelations? Just because those revelations have become familiar doesn't make them any less extraordinary. Every day, we are gifted with the sacrifices of countless other living things (plants, animals, the soil beneath our feet) to sustain our lives. Our own bodies are full of miraculous transformation as we convert food into fuel and oxygen into energy. When Jesus appears, his friends are amazed. Perhaps we can share in a bit of that amazement as we look with awareness and gratitude into our own marvelous, miraculous, surprising lives! Carry your gratitude with you in your time with the children.

Teaching As A Team:

(**Leader 1** has the sandwich)

Leader 2: What do you have there, (name)?

Leader 1: A snack for you.

Leader 2: Thanks, how did you know I was getting hungry? *(takes a bite)* Mmmm, yummy!

Leader 1: Do you know what you're eating there?

Leader 2: *(stops chewing, looks nervous)* PB&J?

Leader 1: Yes, but you're also eating God!

Leader 2: *(looking alarmed, swallows quickly)* God?

Leader 1: Think about it: God makes the grain grow, and

that is made into bread. God also makes the peanuts and the grapes grow, and those are used in the peanut butter and jelly.

Leader 2: Hey, that's true.

Leader 1: God is even inside you right now, helping your body take that sandwich and turn it into energy.

Leader 2: So I can play soccer this afternoon!

Leader 1: Right. You're having lunch with God! Kinda like our story today, when the disciples had lunch with Jesus. Remember, Jesus died and came back from the dead. His friends were still a little spooked by everything, so when they saw him, they were frightened.

Leader 2: It *would* be scary to see someone you thought was dead.

Leader 1: Jesus told them not to worry. He talked and explained things to the disciples. Then he ate lunch with them. Finally, they realized the true miracle of Jesus being there.

Leader 2: What's that?

Leader 1: Not only was Jesus right there with them, but Jesus was going to be with everybody, everywhere, for all time! Every time we eat or drink, every time we breathe in fresh air, and every time we play soccer, Christ is inside us, celebrating life, bringing us love.

Leader 2: *(looking at sandwich in wonder)* Wow. This is one miraculous sandwich!

Leader 1: You said it!

Teaching On Your Own: You know what I have here? It's a snack. I'm getting a little hungry, so if you don't mind... *(take small bite)* Mmmm, yummy. Can you guess what I'm eating here? *(let children guess)* Good guesses. This is a peanut butter and jelly sandwich, but you know what else it is? It's God. I'm eating God! Think about it: God makes the grain grow, and that is made into bread. God also makes the peanuts and the grapes grow, and those are used in the peanut butter and jelly. Even now, as I'm eating the sandwich, God is inside me, helping my body take that sandwich and turn it into energy, so I can play soccer this afternoon. So really, I'm having lunch with God! Isn't that amazing? It's a little like our story today, when the disciples had lunch with Jesus. Remember, Jesus died and came back from the dead. His friends were still a little spooked by everything, so when they saw him, they were frightened. But Jesus told them not to worry. He talked and explained things to the disciples. Then he ate lunch with them. Finally, they realized the true miracle of Jesus being there. Not only was Jesus right there with the disciples, but Jesus was going to be with everybody, everywhere, for all time! Every time we eat or drink, every time we breathe in fresh air, and every time we play soccer, Christ is inside us, celebrating life, bringing us love. You know what that means? This is one miraculous sandwich! And we have miraculous lives, don't we?

Closing Prayer: Thank you, God, for the miracle of our lives and for the blessings of each day. Give us eyes to see you and hearts to love you as we recognize your presence with us every day. In Christ's name we pray, Amen.

Follow-Up Lesson: To reinforce this lesson in a classroom or home setting, plan a fellowship meal for your children. Make sure you have a few different kid-friendly foods (carrots sticks, apple slices, crackers, peanut butter). Ask the children to think about where all these foods came from, and how God was part of their creation. Don't forget to mention all the people (farmers, people in food production, truckers, grocers) who brought this food to us and how God is in all these people as well. Emphasize the miracle of how so many people, places, and nonhuman life is connected in this one snack. Invite the children to eat their snacks prayerfully, thanking God for each bite. You might say a prayer yourself or invite the children to pray for each food item. For a craft, invite the children to think of their favorite things: foods they like to eat, things they like to do, people they love. Give each child a large of poster board (11x14) folded into thirds. At the top of each section, have the children write: "My Favorite Foods," "My Favorite Activities," and "My Favorite People." (If you have small children who can't write, you can do this part in advance.) Then invite the children to write or draw pictures under each category. Write across the entire bottom of the page, "God is in all things!" After the children are done, laminate their projects and encourage them to use them as placemats during meal time to remind them that, with every meal, they are eating with Jesus!

Third Sunday of Easter

1 John 3:1-7

God's Family

Object: Baby pictures (physical or digital)

Babies are so cute. Do you all like babies? (Let them answer.) Look at the baby pictures I brought with me this morning. Wouldn't you agree these babies are cute? (Let them answer.) I don't think I've ever seen a little baby that wasn't cute in his or her own way. That's the way God has made babies.

When a baby is born, he or she becomes a part of a very special group. It's a group that is called a "family." Every family is different. Some are adoptive families. This means that the family "adopts" a baby, because the family sees something special about him or her. The family has chosen this person to be their child. Some are birth families. A birth family is one where the child is born into that family. Some are single-parent families. A single-parent family perhaps has either a father or a mother, but not both. Some families have both a mother and a father. The point is that every family is important to a baby. Could a baby live without a family? (Let them answer.) What do families give babies? (Let them answer.) A baby's family gives him or her food, clothing, and a house to live in. Families are also supposed to give each child love and care.

When we become members of a church, we join another family: the church family. Indeed, we are all called "children of God" because we belong to God. That is how God shows love for us. God calls us "children." We are part of God's own family!

Every one of our families is important. Belonging to God's family and being known as God's child is especially important. That is how God shows love for us. God not only takes care of providing us with air to breathe, water to drink, and food to eat, God also gives us that special ingredient of love.

Dearest God: Thank you for showing your love for us by calling us your children. Amen.

Fourth Sunday of Easter

John 10:11-18

I Am The Good Shepherd

Good morning, boys and girls. Have any of you ever been lost? Were you scared? (Let them answer.) I imagine that if you were lost, your parents stopped whatever they were doing to search for you. They didn't stop searching until they found you. I want to tell you a story this morning about a little boy your age, who was lost. The boy went with his parents to the shopping mall. As the family went from one store to another, there was a mix-up. The boy's father thought the boy was with his mother. The boy's mother thought the boy was with his father. The boy was with neither. He was lost.

The parents immediately stopped what they were doing. They searched and searched for their son. They called the mall security. They checked every store. They talked to all the store managers. Finally, they found their son. The mother and father were like the Good Shepherd in today's lesson. A shepherd is someone who takes care of sheep. A shepherd will do anything to see that his sheep are kept from danger. In today's lesson, Jesus called himself the Good Shepherd. Why do you suppose that Jesus called himself the Good Shepherd? (Let them answer.) The Good Shepherd lays down his life for the sheep. If one of the sheep is missing, the good shepherd will stop what he is doing and go search for the missing sheep. If Jesus is the Good Shepherd, who do you think are his sheep? (Let them answer.) We are Jesus' sheep. A Good Shepherd leads his sheep. If we are sheep and Jesus is our Good Shepherd, then we are to follow Jesus.

The next time you see a lamb or a sheep, remember Jesus. He is the Good Shepherd. He will do anything to keep us safe from harm. We are his sheep.

Prayer: Jesus, thank you for watching over your sheep and caring for us, your children. Help us to look out for each other and to show your love, so that no one will be lost and everyone will be found. Amen.

Fourth Sunday of Easter

1 John 3:16-24

Love By Action!

Object: receipt

Good morning, boys and girls. (Hold up the cash register receipt, ask the question and let them answer.) Do any of you know what this is? You get it at the grocery store. When your parents buy groceries, the person at the cash register puts one of these in your grocery bag. It is called a receipt. It lists everything that you bought at the grocery store. When it is very long, it means that you bought many things.

I want to tell you a story about someone who went to the grocery store and came home with many sacks of groceries. This person's receipt was even longer than mine. The person with the groceries drove into his driveway. He began to take the sacks from the car into the house. While this was going on, next door two children were playing in the yard. The man with the groceries had his house keys in one hand and was trying to carry two large bags up his steps. Suddenly, one sack ripped, and his groceries fell all across the lawn!

The two children saw this happen. One child said to the other, "Our neighbor needs help. Let's go help him pick up his groceries." The other said, "No, let's not. It's not our problem." But the first child ran over and began to pick up groceries. He helped the man carry them into the house. You are probably wondering, "What does this have to do with today's lesson?" Here is the answer: Our lesson tells us to love people by doing something for them, not just by saying we ought to do something. The child who ran over and helped pick up the groceries showed his love for his neighbor by doing something. That's how God wants us to act toward others. This week, I want you to remember to show God's love to others by action. Don't just talk about something — do something for someone else.

Prayer: Dear God, we want to do more than talk about your love. Help us to do the things that will show the world your love. Help us to put your love into action. Amen.

John 15:1-8

Abiding In God

First Thoughts: During these spring months, one descriptor of God comes clear — creativity. God's creative grace is present in the glorious colors of the new flowers, the many shades of green in the newly sprouted trees, the songs of the birds who, returned from their winter homes, now fuss over their hatched offspring. This passage from John tells us that the more we abide in God, the more we become like God. That is, we become fruitful as God is fruitful. We create spaces of beauty in the world with light and splashes of color. Can you see those places in your life, the evidence of God's Spirit living in you? Or perhaps you've been around one of these "glowing" people. What's it like? This is the vision we want to give our children this Sunday, a vision of the Christian life as a reflection of God's glory. As you prepare for this session, invite God's glory to move in your own heart, so the children will catch a glimpse of it in your time together.

Teaching As A Team:

Leader 1: *(looking at Leader 2)* Hey, I know where you've been — the beach!

Leader 2: How did you figure that out? I didn't tell you.

Leader 1: I know, but I can see it on your face.

Leader 2: My face?

Leader 1: Yeah, you've got some pink in your cheeks, and I thought that you probably got that from the sun.

Leader 2: Oh yeah! Hey, why is it that our cheeks look pink when we've been in the sun?

Leader 1: Well, when we're in the sun, our faces kind of soak it up — like sponges. And when we're filled up with it, the sun starts coming out of us, and it makes our cheeks pink.

Leader 2: So it's like I'm a little sun here!

Leader 1: Yeah! It reminds me of our scripture lesson today. Jesus told his friends that if they wanted to be like God, they needed to spend a lot of time with God. They needed to abide in God.

Leader 2: What does it mean to "abide in God"?

Leader 1: Spending time in God. Like you spent time in the sun — you abided in the sun. When we pray or come to church, or sing songs of praise, we're spending time in God. The more we do that, the more we begin to look like God.

Leader 2: Does it make our cheeks pink, like the sun?

Leader 1: Not exactly, but it does show up in our lives. We become more patient, more loving, more kind...

Leader 2: ... more like God.

Leader 1: Exactly.

Leader 2: That's gonna be my new goal — to abide in God so much that when people look at me, they can see God in my life.

Leader 1: Yeah, that's gonna be my goal too!

Teaching On Your Own: *(pink color on face)* Hey, can anybody tell where I went yesterday? Do you see the pink on my cheeks? What usually makes your cheeks pink? Being in the sun, right? So, if my face looks a little pink, then you can probably guess I spent some time in the sun! Can anyone tell me why our cheeks turn pink when we're in the sun? Our faces kind of soak it up — like sponges. When we're filled with the sun, it starts coming out and makes our cheeks pink. That makes us little suns, doesn't it? It reminds me of our scripture lesson today. Jesus told his friends that if they wanted to be like God, they needed to spend a lot of time with God. They needed to abide in God. Do you know what it means to "abide in God"? Abide means to spend time in something. Like when I spend time in the sun — I abide in the sun. When we pray or come to church, or sing songs of praise, we're spending time in God, abiding in God. The more we do that, the more we begin to look like God. Now it doesn't make our cheeks pink, like the sun. But it does show up in our lives. We become more patient, more loving, more kind... more like God. You know what? That's gonna be my new goal — to abide in God so much that when people look at me, they can see God in my life. In fact, why don't we all make that our goal?

Closing Prayer: God, help us to abide in you, to become so full of you that it shows up in our lives. We want to be your light in the world, and to help others know your love and your grace. In Christ's name we pray, Amen.

Follow-Up Lesson: To reinforce this lesson in a classroom or home environment, spend some time introducing the children to the different fruits of the Spirit as listed in Galatians 5: love, joy, peace, forbearance, kindness, goodness, faithfulness, gentleness, and self-control. Give them a chance to think about how these gifts manifest in our lives. Give them a chance to identify the places where they already manifest these gifts, and areas where they'd like to grow more. For a craft, create a big tree on some poster board to hang on the wall. On the branches, write different things we can do to abide in God: read the Bible, pray, worship at church, sing songs, and spend time being quiet with God. Give each child a few different cut-out shapes of fruits (red apples, purple grapes, yellow lemons, and so forth). Invite the children to pick the fruits of the Spirit they most respond to and write the name of the gift on the fruit. Then beneath the name of the fruit include a live example of it in the world. Decorate the tree with the children's fruits and leave it in the classroom as a reminder of our goal to abide in God and grow in the Spirit.

Fifth Sunday of Easter

1 John 4:7-21

God Is Love

Good morning, boys and girls. Have you ever thrown anyone a kiss? (Let them answer.) When you throw someone a kiss, it means that you love that person. You love that person, even though you can't see the kiss that you throw. My children and I throw each other kisses. Here's how we do it. (Demonstrate throwing a kiss from the palm of your hand.) I want to tell you a story about a boy who went to visit his grandparents for a weekend. When he left his home, his parents threw him a kiss, but he put the kiss in his pocket. (While you tell this, follow the actions you describe.)

He arrived at his grandparent's house and finally went to bed. Before he turned out the light, he took the kiss from his pocket and put it on his cheek. Has that ever happened to you? (Let them answer.) When you throw someone a kiss, it is invisible. You can't see it. Even so, you know that it is there. The boy kept his kiss in his pocket all day and used it at night.

Invisible kisses are like God. The Bible says that no one has ever seen God. It also says that if we love one another, God lives in us. God is like an invisible kiss, isn't God? No one has ever seen a kiss that you throw, but you know that the kiss is there. If you are like the boy, the kiss lives in your pocket until you need it.

The next time you throw a kiss to someone, remember God. No one has ever seen God. If we love one another, God lives in us. God is like a kiss we throw. We can't see the kiss we throw, but we know that it is there.

Prayer: God, let us catch an air kiss from you (reach out a hand to grab a kiss from the air). And now, we will share that kiss with the world (throw out an imaginary kiss from your hand). Help us to think about ways in which we can share your love every day. Amen.

Sixth Sunday of Easter

John 15:9-17

Jesus Chose You

Object: invitations

Good morning, boys and girls. Do you know what the word "choose" means? (Let them answer.) Choosing means "to pick out something", like one cookie on a whole plate of cookies. When you take that cookie, you are choosing.

I love to go to the ice cream store that has all kinds of flavors in a big case, like butter pecan, chocolate, mint, moose tracks, caramel, and vanilla, and thirty more different kinds. I think I will choose black cherry ice cream but then I look some more and I think I will choose chocolate fudge. But it is hard, because there are so many other flavors. There is superman ice cream and raspberry sherbet, but I have to make a choice. I can't make one choice, so I get a double dipper of butter pecan and moose tracks. Choosing two kinds out of 39 isn't bad, is it? (Let them answer.)

Jesus said he made choices, also. According to the Bible, Jesus chose you. He said very plainly that we did not choose him, but instead Jesus chose us. Does that make you feel good? (Let them answer.)

When you play games like kickball or dodgeball, are you happy when someone chooses you to be on their team? (Let them answer.) The team leader chooses you because he/she believes you are a good kickball player, or a good dodgeball player. The leader thinks you are a good kicker or a good dodger. The leader wants the best players on his/her team.

Jesus chose you. He thinks you will make a good disciple. Jesus chose you to go and make other disciples. A disciple is chosen because he/she has a lot of love to share with others. A disciple makes friends and talks to them about the Bible and how to forgive. A disciple shares things that belong to him/her when a friend needs help. A disciple cares for people that are lonely or sick.

I brought some invitations with me today. (Show the invitations.) This invitation is from Jesus. Jesus invites you to be one of his very own. Jesus chose you to be all of the things a good disciple is, and to be a friend of Jesus.

Is this special? (Let them answer.) It is special to be chosen by Jesus and something we should always remember. We did not choose Jesus, but instead Jesus chose us. (Hand out the invitations.) I want you take your invitation home and put it on your dresser. Whenever you see the invitation, you will always remember that Jesus chose you to be one of his disciples. Amen.

Prayer: Thank you, Jesus, for choosing us to be your disciples. Each of us is different, and you have special things for us to do. Thank you for choosing us to be on your team. We will work and play together as we reach out to the world with your love. Amen.

1 John 5:1-6

House Rules

Object: list of house rules

Good morning, boys and girls. How many of you brushed your teeth this morning before coming to church? (Let them answer.) Good, who told you to brush your teeth? (Let them answer.) How many of you wash your hands before eating? (Let them answer.) Very good, your mom or your dad tells you to wash your hands. Who tells you what time to go to bed, say your prayers, and turns out the light? (Let them answer.) Mom and Dad!

I have a list of some rules to show you. (Show them the list.) I call these "House Rules," and they are very important rules because they help us get along at home. Everyone knows that they must brush their teeth, wash their hands, eat at the table, go to bed at a certain time, say their prayers, and get a good night's sleep. What happens when you don't do these things? (Let them answer.) People get pretty unhappy, don't they? Sometimes we end up saying things that we don't mean and sometimes we even end up crying and being sent to our room, don't we? (Let them answer.) But most of the time, we do what we know we are supposed to do, and when we do everything, it is wonderful. Our homes are filled with love, aren't they? (Let them answer.)

God has rules for his family also. What do we call God's rules? (Let them answer.) Very good, we call them commandments and we obey his commandments because we love God, and we love being a part of his family.

God's commandments are filled with love. His commandments teach us to love our parents, to say good things about one another, and to respect each other's property and each other's body. We encourage each other to do well and to share with people who have problems and need help. God teaches us how important the truth is and how important the big family of God is to one another.

At home, we have rules and those rules make our families happy. After a while, no one even has to tell us to brush our teeth, tell the truth, wash our hands, eat at the table, say our prayers, and go to bed on time. We do it because we know it makes us happy and filled with love. But first, we have to learn the rules. It is the same in God's family. Once we learn the commandments and understand how happy it makes everyone when we keep them, then we just keep on doing them because of the love it brings.

The next time your mom or dad asks you if you brushed your teeth or washed your hands, you will know that you are being asked to follow the rules. If you do, it will help you have a happy family. If you keep God's commandments, your life will be filled with love and you will be part of God's very big and happy family.

Prayer: God, sometimes we don't follow rules because we think that we would have more fun without them. Remind us, God, that all of your commandments are there to help us. Thank you, God, for such good rules. Amen.

Luke 24:44-53

Sent Out As Christ

First Thoughts: As we enter this celebration of Ascension and prepare for Pentecost, we're going to use this lesson to focus on the mission of the church. Because we know that when Christ ascended, it wasn't the end of God's mission on earth, but a new beginning. We are able to understand something the early disciples struggled with, which is that the kingdom of God wasn't going to come through Jesus' efforts alone, but through the faithful commitment of his followers. It's important for us to keep in mind that Jesus' actual ministry involved only a small area of the world. It was the ministry and commitment of the church's early leaders that spread the gospel message; men and women like us who gave their lives to sharing God's message of healing and peace. It's a mission we've inherited, and one we pass onto our children. What does it mean for your church to carry the gospel message into the world? How about you personally? Carry this reflection — and its challenge — with you in your time with the children.

Teaching As A Team:

*(**Leader** 2 has a bag of cookies.)*

Leader 1: Mmm, something smells good. What's that in your bag, (name)?

Leader 2: It's my grandma's cookies.

Leader 1: But I thought your grandma wasn't alive anymore.

Leader 2: You're right. My grandmother died five years ago.

Leader 1: Then how do you have her cookies?

Leader 2: Oh, well, I have her recipe book. So whenever I'm feeling sad, missing my grandmother, or whenever I want to make the best cookies in the world, I just pull out the recipe book and make a treat. It makes me kinda feel like she's still here.

Leader 1: You're right — she kinda is. When you cook one of her recipes, you're keeping a piece of her alive. It reminds me of our scripture passage today, when Jesus returned to heaven. Remember just a few weeks ago we talked about how Jesus died and was resurrected?

Leader 2: Yeah, then he spent some time with his friends.

Leader 1: Well now is the time when Jesus leaves them again. He's returning to heaven now, but this time things are different. Before the disciples were scared and sad, because they saw him die on the cross. This time they understand something important — the kingdom of God is still growing and spreading.

Leader 2: But how can it if Jesus isn't around to teach and heal people?

Leader 1: Because Jesus told them *they* would be the ones to teach and to heal, and lead people to God's love. Jesus told them that they would be filled with God's power and do many great things and — since there were several of them, the message would spread to more people much more quickly than if Jesus did it by himself.

Leader 2: So, really, once Jesus went back to heaven, things *really* got started.

Leader 1: Right, and God asks us to do the same things today — teaching about Jesus and sharing God's love. And now there are millions of us!

Leader 2: Sharing God's love. I guess that's what really reaches people.

Leader 1: Right, sharing. For example, if you were to share your grandma's cookies...

Leader 2: You could all share in her memory! That's a great idea. *(gives Leader 1 a cookie)*

Leader 1: Yum. I totally agree!

Teaching On Your Own: Hey, guys. Do you smell something yummy? *(sniff at bag)* Mmm, it's coming from my bag. You know what's in here? My grandma's cookies! Now my grandmother died five years ago, so how do you think I have her cookies? I have her recipe book. So whenever I'm feeling sad, missing my grandmother, or whenever I want to make the best cookies in the world, I just pull out the recipe book and make a treat. It makes me kinda feel like she's still here. Like I'm keeping a piece of her alive. It reminds me of our scripture passage today, when Jesus returned to heaven. Remember just a few weeks ago, we talked about how Jesus died and was resurrected? Well, now is the time when Jesus leaves his friends behind again. He's returning to heaven now, but this time things are different. Before the disciples were scared and sad, because they saw him die on the cross. This time, they understand something important — the kingdom of God is still growing and spreading. But now it won't be Jesus teaching and healing and sharing God's love with everybody. Now it will be all of Jesus' friends. Jesus told them that they would be filled with God's power and do many great things and, since there were several of them — the message would spread to more people much more quickly than if Jesus did it by himself. So, really, once Jesus went back to heaven, things *really* got started. And God asks us to do the same things today — teaching about Jesus and sharing God's love. And now there are millions of us! Sharing God's love. That's what really reaches people. And that's just what I'm going to do with these cookies — share them! Then ,you can all see what a sweet person my grandma was, inside and out.

Closing Prayer: Help us, God, to carry your message of love and peace into the world. We realize that we are your hands, your feet, and your heart in the world. Help us to be the little Christs you have called us to be. In Christ's name we pray, Amen.

Follow-Up Lesson: To reinforce this lesson in a home or classroom setting, spend time revisiting some of Jesus' teachings. Pick three or four of Jesus' parables that you're familiar with, and summarize them for the children (the good Samaritan, the prodigal son, the lost sheep, and so forth). Ask the children to identify what Jesus is teaching us. Then ask the children how they can apply these lessons to their own lives. Finally, as a craft project, help the children create their own gospel recipe book. In advance, you can print out a title page for their book, along with additional pages inside depicting the parables (perhaps using coloring pages). Or, you can simply provide blank pages and allow the children to do all the illustrating themselves. Encourage the children to write the lesson at the bottom of each page ("Be a good neighbor," "God loves us no matter what we do," and so on). Ask the children how they might use this recipe book to stay close to God and to help them keep Christ alive in their own lives and in the world.

Ascension of the Lord

Ephesians 1:15-23

Jesus The Head

What would you think of a doll that didn't have a head? (Let them answer.) Would you play with a doll like this much? (Let them answer.) I doubt it. Dolls should have their heads — just like people must have their heads. The head is an important part of our bodies. We couldn't live without our heads. We could live without our feet, hands, legs, or arms, but we absolutely must have our heads.

Today, we learned that the church also has a head. Can you tell me the head of the church? (Let them answer.) Jesus is the head of the church. Any church that does not realize that Jesus is its head is like this headless doll. It is not a real church. The real church operates with Jesus as the head.

Just how do you think Jesus operates as the head of the church? Please share with me your thoughts. (Let them answer.)

Let's look at it another way. Jesus is our boss. If we had a job and were paid for what we did, we would probably have someone who is our boss. The boss makes the decisions about what should be done and when and where and how. This boss is in charge.

In the same way, Jesus is our boss here at this church. We do things that Jesus wants us to do — at least we try to.

Dearest Lord Jesus: Thank you for taking charge and for being the head and boss of the church. Amen.

Seventh Sunday of Easter

John 17:6-19

Protect Them

"Holy Father, protect them in your name...." (John 17:11a)

Object: glove

Hello children,

I'm so glad to see you this morning. How are you? (Let them answer.) Notice, I have something on my hand. What is it? (Children answer — "a glove.")

Yes, it's a glove, and I am wearing it for a special reason.

And the special reason is to demonstrate a very important truth.

So what does a glove do? Its main purpose is to protect. This glove protects my hand from hurt and harm. It protects my hand from the cold. This amazing glove protects from cuts, bruises, and injuries. (Presenter speaks to the glove.) "Thank you glove, for protecting my hand."

Jesus was going away. He would not be with his disciples any more. So Jesus prayed a *protection prayer.* He asked God to protect his disciples.

"Protect them," he says, "from the evil one. Protect them and guard them from choosing wrong paths. Protect them from sin."

How do you think Jesus' disciples felt when they learned that Jesus was going away? How did they feel knowing Jesus and was praying for them? (Let them answer.) How do people feel when they learn they are being thought of and prayed for?

You and I can pray protection prayers too.

Let's take this glove and let it guide us in praying protection prayers for others.

(Presenter points to each finger on the glove as he/she speaks.)

Let the thumb represent praying for others as our neighbors, church, and nation.

Let the pointer finger represent our teachers who point the way.

Let the large middle finger represent our leaders and all in authority.

Let the ring finger represent marriage, and family.

Let the little finger represent the "little people" that is, the poor, the weak, the hungry.

Prayer: Holy Father, protect others. Protect our teachers. Protect our leaders. Protect families. Protect the little ones, as Jesus prayed protection for his disciples. Amen.

Seventh Sunday of Easter

1 John 5:9-13

God's Testimony

Object: picture of random person, videotape, book

Good morning! Imagine this is a picture of a famous person who lived and died and who some believe never even existed. Let's say his name is "Adam Zoe." (Show the children a picture of a person.) Now I could say, "I know Adam Zoe existed because this picture proves it." We could say that a picture gives "testimony" about a person. It says something about a person. The problem with a picture, however, is that the picture could be of anyone! How could anyone know for sure this is a picture of Adam Zoe?

"Oh," I might say, "I've also got a videotape of this person to prove that he really did live at one time." (Show the children the videotape.) I could say this videotape gives "testimony" about a person.

I could also say that this book is a book about the life of Adam Zoe. It also gives "testimony" that Adam Zoe lived.

All these things indicate the truth that a man named Adam Zoe lived. But none of them really prove the point so much as one other "testimony." What would that be? (Let them answer.) It would be the "testimony" of a person who actually knew Adam Zoe. Let's say I'm that person. If I knew him and could tell others about him, that would be a powerful proof or "testimony" about Adam Zoe, wouldn't it?

When John wrote his letter to the early Christians, he talked about "testimony" and said that the strongest "testimony" or proof of who Jesus was and what Jesus did came from God! Since God says that Jesus is real and that Jesus' ministry was exactly what he said it was, we know that Jesus is true and real. We have the "testimony" of God! That's better than an eyewitness, a book, a videotape, or a photograph!

God's testimony about Jesus is that we have eternal life because of Jesus. Isn't that wonderful? I'm so glad we have God's proof; God's testimony!

Dearest Lord God: Thank you for your testimony about Jesus. We believe. Amen.

www.ingramcontent.com/pod-product-compliance
Lightning Source LLC
LaVergne TN
LVHW050939080826
845145LV00004B/1327

* 9 7 8 0 7 8 8 0 3 0 4 0 6 *